THE GREAT RACE: FIGHT TO THE FINISH

# BUILDING THE TRANSCONTINENTAL RAILROAD

## RACE OF THE RAILROAD COMPANIES

KELLY WITTMANN

Gareth Stevens PUBLISHING

Please visit our website, www.garethstevens.com.
For a free color catalog of all our high-quality books,
call toll free 1-800-542-2595 or fax 1-877-542-2596.

CATALOGING-IN-PUBLICATION DATA

Names: Wittmann, Kelly.
Title: Building the transcontinental railroad: race of the railroad companies / Kelly Wittmann.
Description: New York : Gareth Stevens Publishing, 2018. | Series: The great race: fight to the finish | Includes index.
Identifiers: ISBN 9781538208267 (pbk.) | ISBN 9781538208168 (library bound) | ISBN 9781538208045 (6 pack)
Subjects: LCSH: Pacific railroads--History--Juvenile literature. | Railroads--United States--History--Juvenile literature. | Railroads--West (U.S.)--History--Juvenile literature.
Classification: LCC TF25.P23 W57 2018 | DDC 385.0978--dc23

Published in 2018 by
**Gareth Stevens Publishing**
111 East 14th Street, Suite 349
New York, NY 10003

**Developed and Produced by Focus Strategic Communications, Inc.**

Project Manager: Adrianna Edwards
Editor: Ron Edwards
Layout and Composition: Ruth Dwight
Copy editors: Adrianna Edwards, Francine Geraci
Media Researchers: Adrianna Edwards, Paula Joiner, Maddi Nixon
Proofreader: Francine Geraci
Index: Ron Edwards, Maddi Nixon

PHOTO CREDITS
Credit Abbreviations: **G** Getty; **LOC** Library of Congress; **NARA** National Archives and Records Administration; **S** Shutterstock; **WC** Wikimedia Commons

Position on the page: **T:** top, **B:** bottom, **L:** left, **R:** right

**Cover: G**: Wolfgang Kaehler; **4:** NARA/513348; **5:** Historical Postcard showing harbor in Bridgeport, Connecticut/WC; **6:** LOC/LC-DIG-pga-07643; **7:** Everett Historical/S; **8:** Darios/S; **9:** Marzolino/S; **10:** Radoslaw Lecyk/S; **11:** © Frank Schulenburg/CC BY-SA 3.0; **12:** Patricia Hofmeester/S; **13:** Petr Levicek/S; **14:** Everett Historical/S; **15:** LOC/LC-USZ62-63955; **16:** Depiano/S; **17:** LOC/LC-USZC4-3595; **18:** Everett Historical/S; **19:** Everett Historical/S; **20:** Joseph Sohm/S; **21:** Everett Historical/S; **22:** LOC/LC-USZC6-57; **23:** LOC/LC-DIG-cwpbh-00631; **24:** Everett Historical/S; **25:** Nicolas Primola/S; **26:** Heartland Arts/S; **27:** LOC/LC-USZ62-16530; **28:** Ragne Kabanova/S; 29: LOC/LC-DIG-pga-07237; **30:** LOC/LC-USZ62-77909; **31:** LOC/LC-DIG-cwpb-01063; **32:** LOC/LC-DIG-ppmsca-17158; **33:** NARA/535159; **35:** Marzolino/S; **36:** OLOS/S; **37:** NARA/594940; **38:** turtix/S; **39:** Joe+Jeanette Archie/WC; **40:** LOC/LC-DIG-highsm-13375; **41:** villorejo/S; **42:** Futhark_TKA/S; **43:** LOC/LC-USZ62-66462; **44:** Felix Lipov/S.



Printed in the United States of America
CPSIA compliance information: Batch CS17GS: For further information contact Gareth Stevens, New York, New York at 1-800-542-2595.

# CONTENTS

# THE PASSION OF THEODORE JUDAH

On November 2, 1863, a young man lay in a hotel room on Wall Street in New York City, suffering greatly from the yellow fever he had contracted while crossing the Isthmus of Panama. His name was Theodore Judah. Knowing that he stood at death's doorstep, he must have thought back on his life and wondered where it had all gone wrong.

Wall Street was a busy place in 1867.

## WALL STREET

In the 1860s, Wall Street was the center of America's **financial sector**, just as it is today. The business on Wall Street not only affected the lives of all Americans, but the lives of many other people all over the world.

## A HAPPY START

Theodore Judah was born in Bridgeport, Connecticut, on March 4, 1826. He was known as "Ted" to family and friends. The son of an Episcopal minister, Judah led a fairly privileged life and had the opportunity to get a good education.

This historical postcard shows a view of the harbor in Bridgeport, Connecticut.

## AMBITION

Other young men of the **Victorian era** might have amused themselves with trivial sporting events and parties. But Judah was a serious person who was interested in engineering from an early age. After graduating from Rensselaer Polytechnic Institute, he was in great demand by the railroad companies of the Northeast. However, his ambition was even larger than the opportunities that they could provide.

## QUEEN VICTORIA AND THE VICTORIAN ERA

Though Queen Victoria was only the ruler of Great Britain and its colonies, the phrase "Victorian era" is used to describe the period from 1837 to 1901 anywhere in the English-speaking world and beyond. The queen's political and personal lives influenced many Americans.

This 1859 portrait by German painter Franz Xavier Winterhalter shows Queen Victoria at about age 40.

# A BOLD PLAN

In 1854, the president of the Sacramento Valley Railroad, William Tecumseh Sherman, and his associates summoned Judah to New York City. They told him they wanted him to go to California to help build the Sacramento Valley Line. It would have been much easier and more profitable for Judah to simply stay in the Northeast and continue to build railroads there, but Judah's ambition overcame his doubts. He headed off for the "Wild West."

After building the Sacramento Valley Railroad, William Tecumseh Sherman (shown here) went on to serve as a Union general in the Civil War.

## CALIFORNIA-BOUND

When Judah went to California, his mind was already racing far ahead of his bosses' plans. He knew what he really wanted to do: build the first transcontinental railroad. He made no secret of this plan. Because land travel from the East to California was too time-consuming, Judah and his wife had a daunting journey by boat ahead of them. They sailed south through the Gulf of Mexico and the Caribbean Sea, then headed west through a river in Nicaragua, and then north to San Francisco.

## SAN FRANCISCO

In the 1850s, San Francisco was a rapidly growing **boomtown**. The California gold rush began in 1848 and caused the population of San Francisco to explode from 1,000 to 25,000 in under a year. Between gold mining and the building of the transcontinental railroad, many businesses were founded to serve the influx of workers, including jeans manufacturer Levi Strauss & Co.

The heavy denim the company used, held together by patented copper rivets, was a big hit with those who did heavy labor.

## ON TO THE NEXT DREAM

Building the Sacramento Valley Railroad Line was a huge accomplishment because it was the first railroad west of the Mississippi River. But at its completion in 1856, Judah was eager to get started on his dream project. He began planning for a great Pacific railroad — one that would stretch across the entire American West. He was so enthusiastic and loud in his boasting that he became known as "Crazy Judah."

The great Pacific railroad, or the Union Pacific, took hard manual labor to complete.

## OBSTACLES

One thing that stood in the way of the new railroad was the Sierra Nevada mountain range. Running 400 miles (644 km) north to south and 70 miles (113 km) east to west, the Sierra Nevada seemed insurmountable. Its enormous cliffs of granite had been formed by volcanic activity and **glacial** cutting over millions of years. But when Judah climbed Donner Pass, he found the answer — a place where the Pacific road could safely climb and descend.

Mount Whitney is located in the Eastern Sierra Nevada Mountains. With an elevation of 14,505 feet (4,420 m), it is the highest summit in the Sierra Nevada range and in the southern United States.

This is a view of Donner Lake from Donner Pass.

## DONNER PASS

Donner Pass was named after a group of pioneers who were trying to reach California in November of 1846. The Donner party started out on their journey like many others, traveling by wagon. They became trapped by heavy snow while climbing through the Sierra Nevada range. When they ran out of food and began to starve, some in the party resorted to **cannibalism**. Of the nearly 90 members of the Donner party, only about 45 made it to California alive.

## SAD END

Sadly, it wasn't long before the transcontinental railroad project began to go wrong. People with less-than-pure intentions often try to steal the ideas of young, ambitious geniuses. Though Judah seemed worldly and experienced, he could still be **naïve** and too trusting of associates. Before he knew it, he found himself flat on his bed in New York City, his life slowly slipping away. Who were the people who drove him to this end? And what were the ideas that influenced them in their quest for power?

### YELLOW FEVER

Though a very effective vaccine now exists to prevent yellow fever, 30,000 to 60,000 people still die from it every year, just as Theodore Judah did.

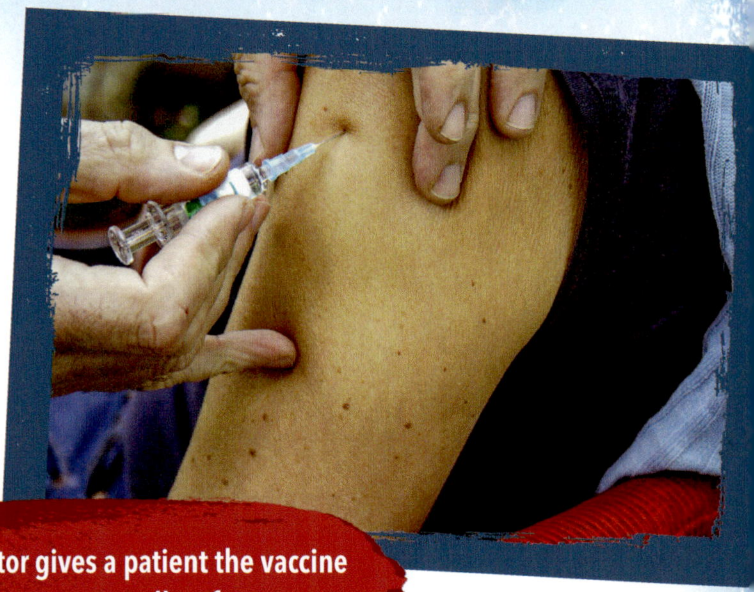

A doctor gives a patient the vaccine to prevent yellow fever.

# THE POWER PLAYERS

Theodore Judah was just one of many men who were interested in building a transcontinental railroad. A railroad that spanned the country would mean economic expansion. It would mean that the people who made products could ship them to more consumers. Pioneers who had endured many hardships in order to settle the West now wanted to have some of the material comforts that Easterners enjoyed. Factory owners who produced all kinds of goods were the suppliers who wanted to fulfill this demand.

Farm tools, cooking utensils, and fabrics were in high demand by pioneers who settled the West.

This photo shows the interior of an old general store in Idaho.

## GENERAL STORES

The general store was where people in the eighteenth and nineteenth centuries bought goods. In the American West, settlers bought goods that were shipped from the East. Those things could not be shipped easily when the means of transportation was slow-moving wagons. The merchants who owned the general stores clamored for railroads that could bring more goods more quickly.

## NOTHING CAME EASILY

But even though there were calls to build a transcontinental railroad coming from all sides, Theodore Judah knew it wouldn't be an easy process. He knew he would have to convince investors in order to raise the money he needed to build it. Luckily, he had spent much time doing what we would now call **networking**. A merchant named Collis Huntington offered to find these investors for Judah.

Collis Potter Huntington was an influential figure in the building of several railroads across the United States.

### FAST FACT

Business networking in the nineteenth century often took place in what were called "gentlemen's clubs." By definition, these clubs excluded women. They made it very difficult for both women and people of color to break into business.

## THE BIG FOUR

The four investors — Collis Huntington, Charles Crocker, Mark Hopkins, and Leland Stanford — were called "The Big Four." They were all wealthy merchants. Each made an initial investment of $1,500 (over $40,000 today). Like all investors, then and now, they were looking to make a good return on what they had deposited. The pressure was on for Judah to make a success of this business venture. It came to be known as the Central Pacific Railroad.

## WOMEN IN THE WEST

Once out West, Judah was supported in his work by his wife, Anna. Life for women in the West was very hard, and many of them who contributed greatly to help build the United States have been unjustly left out of history.

**Corsets, hoop skirts, and bustles were staples of Victorian era fashion and were usually a sign of status. In the mid-1800s, hoop skirts were popular with wealthy and working-class women alike.**

## WHAT ABOUT WASHINGTON?

Investors weren't the only ones who needed convincing. Judah and his new associates knew that they would have to convince those in Washington, DC, too. Private businesses can't just do whatever they want. There are laws and regulations that must be followed. So the newly formed board of the Central Pacific Railroad presented their plan to lawmakers at the nation's capital.

This is an early photograph of the United States Capitol in Washington, DC, 1846. The building is the home for the United States Congress, the legislative branch of the federal government.

## CIVIL WAR

The Pacific Railroad Act was approved by the House of Representatives on May 6, 1862, and by the Senate on June 20, and was signed into law by President Abraham Lincoln on July 1. The fact that the Civil War was raging at the time actually made the passage of this act easier because Northerners were much more open to federal projects than Southerners. The South distrusted the federal government and had prevented the passage of a transcontinental railroad bill in 1856.

The Battle of Shiloh was a major battle during the Civil War. It was fought in 1862 in southwestern Tennessee.

Abraham Lincoln was the sixteenth president of the United States, from March 4, 1861, until his assassination on April 15, 1865.

## ABRAHAM LINCOLN

Many people marveled at Abraham Lincoln's resolve to build a railroad at the same time as he was fighting a civil war. But the president had always believed in the power of will. He once told a friend in a letter, "Always bear in mind that your own **resolution** to succeed is more important than any other one thing."

## THE WAR'S LONG REACH

Though the Civil War was being fought in the Eastern half of the American continent, its effects were felt far beyond its technical borderlines. Southern **legislators** did not want their people going west to "free states" because they feared that would hurt the South and strengthen the Union. The fewer people they had in their Southern states, the less money in taxes they could raise, and the fewer soldiers they could recruit for their cause.

**Before the railroad was built, people traveled to the West in wagon trains such as this.**

## WORKING TOGETHER

Though the South did what it could to stop migration to the West, ultimately Civil War veterans from both the Union and Confederate sides worked on the building of the first transcontinental railroad.

This photo shows the Central Pacific Railroad construction on the upper slope of Prospect Hill in the Sierra Nevada Mountains, about 1867.

## BRINGING THE STATES TOGETHER

California had been a state only since 1850, and some people there wanted to secede with the South. President Abraham Lincoln believed that a transcontinental railroad would cement California's relationship with the Union. He was eager to get the job done.

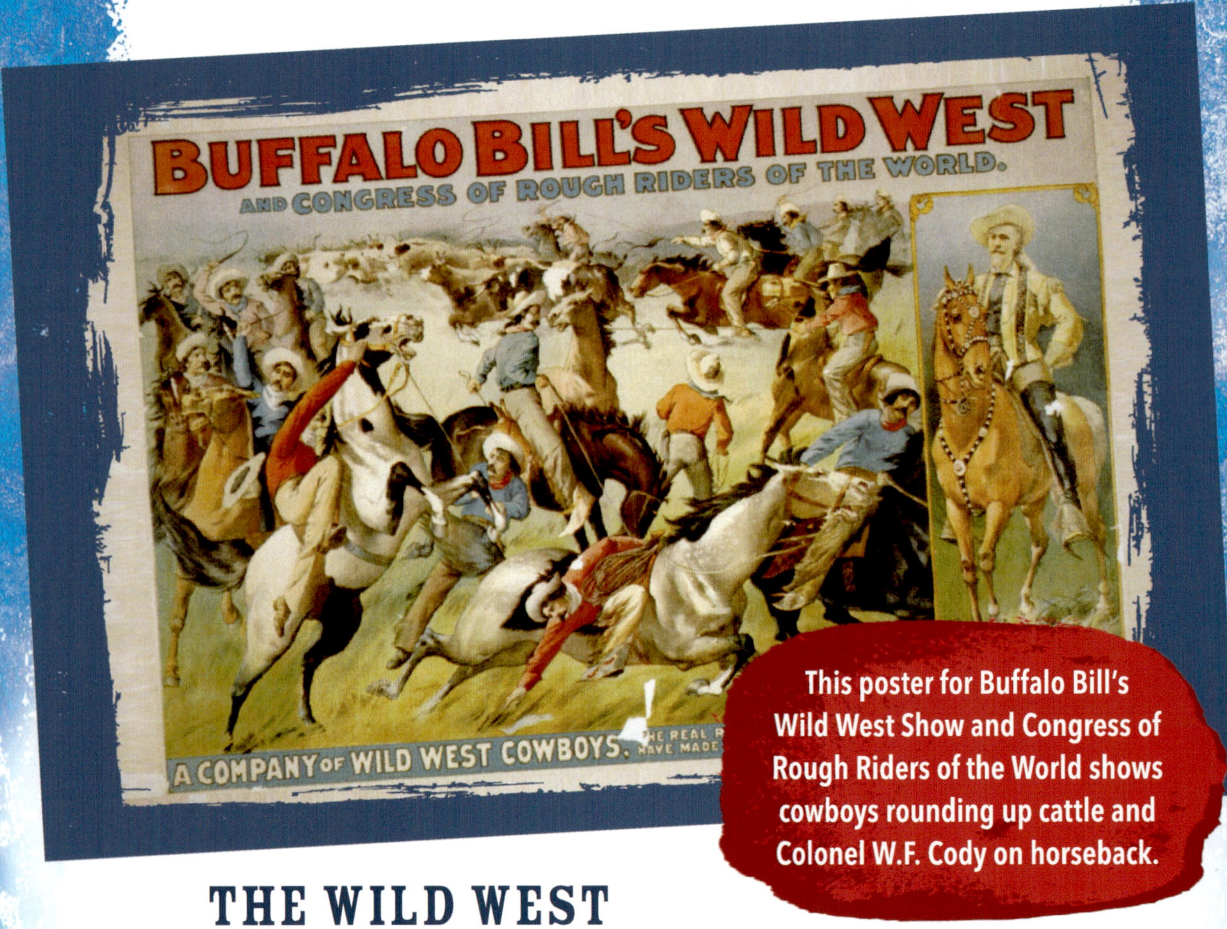


This poster for Buffalo Bill's Wild West Show and Congress of Rough Riders of the World shows cowboys rounding up cattle and Colonel W.F. Cody on horseback.

## THE WILD WEST

California was part of what was called "The Wild West." One of the reasons it was called that is that government authority was loose and undefined. It was land that was up for grabs, by whomever could get there and take control first.

## TWO TRACKS

The Pacific Railroad Act created two main railroad lines: the Central Pacific spanning the West from California, and the Union Pacific from the East. They were to meet in Utah. This gave the companies that ran them government bonds and land grants. From Sacramento, California, and Omaha, Nebraska, these two lines would be built running toward each other to meet in the middle. Things were going as well as they possibly could for the Big Four.

## OAKES AMES

Oakes Ames, a Republican congressman from Massachusetts, was a driving force behind the Union Pacific Railroad. But he used his influence to gain contracts for his family's construction business, and sold company shares to friends at prices far below market value. As a result, Congress censured him in 1873, and the press branded him "Hoax Ames."

Oakes Ames learned the dangers of mixing politics and business.

## BETRAYAL

Theodore Judah also came to grief in the wake of the railroad's success. Almost as soon as the Central Pacific Railroad got the go-ahead from lawmakers, the Big Four began to turn on him. Judah was ultimately betrayed by his associates when they put contractor Charles Crocker in charge of construction. They went ahead and used Judah's plans almost down to the last detail for their own glory. This was a heartbreaking demotion for Judah.

Charles Crocker is credited with the founding of the Central Pacific Railroad.

# THE IDEAS AND THE EFFECTS

The two **ideologies** that drove the building of the transcontinental railroad were **capitalism** and **Manifest Destiny**. Capitalism is an economic system that focuses on the individual, not groups of people. Capitalism favors privately owned businesses rather than state-run or cooperative means of production. Though various forms of capitalistic systems had been in place in the Western world since the fourteenth century, it took a long time for people to study it and name it.

## FEUDALISM

Before European societies began adopting capitalism, most people lived under **feudalism**. In that system, people traded their labor for the right to live on the land of a wealthy nobleman.

This image depicts the work that those of the lower class would have to do while a nobleman looked on.

## ADAM SMITH

Most historians agree that Adam Smith, a Scottish philosopher, was the first to describe capitalism in his 1776 work, *The Wealth of Nations*. Smith argued that if individual producers were left alone by the government, they would instinctively adjust their output to consumers in a way that would benefit society as a whole. He described this as "the system of natural liberty." He is now referred to by many as the "father of capitalism."

**Influenced by Aristotle, Hume, Locke, Voltaire, and other great thinkers, Adam Smith's theories of economics also live on. This monument to Adam Smith is located in Edinburgh, Scotland.**

## NAMING THE SYSTEM

Around the same time that the railroad industry underwent an explosion of growth, this idea of "capitalism" came into being with the **Industrial Revolution**. The first known use of the English word "capitalism" was in an 1854 novel, *The Newcomers*, by William Makepeace Thackeray. In the next decade, the German **communist** philosopher Karl Marx would publish *Das Kapital*, which criticized the capitalist process of production. Marx believed that capitalism ultimately benefited none but the ruling class, and that the only way for workers ever to get fair treatment was to organize against business owners.

## KARL MARX

Karl Marx's alternative to capitalism — communism — caused much suffering in the Soviet Union and in many other countries. When people are thought of only as members of a group, the civil rights of individuals are often violated. The communist Soviet Union lasted from 1922 to 1991.

**Marxism is the school of thought based on Karl Marx's theories.**

## EFFECTS OF CAPITALISM

History has shown that capitalism has both positive and negative effects, depending on its environment and how it is exercised. Just as many American pioneers of the nineteenth century wanted to move west in order to make their fortune, many immigrants to the United States today believe the nation's capitalistic system offers them the best shot at financial comfort.

However, capitalism becomes abusive when pure profit is put ahead of the lives of human beings. Many workers today are being abused in sweatshops all around the world.

Sweatshops are able to produce an abundance of product because workers are paid very little and must work long hours in poor working conditions.

## DESTINY OR DESTRUCTION?

Manifest Destiny, a term coined by journalist John O'Sullivan in 1845, was the idea that American notions of development were superior and could correct the societal problems found in Europe. Early proponents of Manifest Destiny believed in spreading their dream through peaceful, nonviolent means. But the combination of Manifest Destiny and capitalism meant that profit often triumphed over people.

**Decades before the transcontinental railroad, President Andrew Jackson used the idea of Manifest Destiny to force Native Americans from their tribal lands to reservations in the Midwest. Thousands died on the Trail of Tears in 1838.**

## CONSEQUENCES

Though capitalism and Manifest Destiny improved the lives of some people (mostly white Americans), other groups suffered when these ideas were brought into reality through the construction of the transcontinental railroad. Native Americans, whose lands were systematically taken from them by the US government, were devastated by this and other such projects.

Mexico had lost huge amounts of its territory in the Mexican-American War of 1846–1848, including nearly all of modern California, New Mexico, Arizona, Nevada, and Utah. Mexicans were further hurt by railroad expansion. Between 10,000 and 15,000 Chinese immigrants worked on the Central Pacific Railroad, and many labored in very dangerous working conditions. Hundreds died. Irish immigrants also suffered many of the same indignities.

After being displaced by the building of the transcontinental railroad, Native Americans were put on display as curiosities for the entertainment of fairgoers at the 1876 Centennial Exposition in Philadelphia.

# CONSTRUCTION OF A CONTINENT

The building of the transcontinental railroad would need the brainpower of the finest technological minds of the mid-nineteenth century. College-educated engineers and surveyors were hired to begin planning and mapping the railroad routes of the Central Pacific and the Union Pacific.

Gathering the best and brightest to work on the construction of the transcontinental railroad was made difficult by the fact that the Civil War had thrown many college campuses into chaos. Northern colleges saw an exodus of Southern students who had to return home to serve in the Confederate Army. Many Southern colleges were turned into army hospitals.

Field hospitals such as this took care of the injured after a Civil War battle.

## FROM ALL ACROSS THE LAND

Many of the men who worked on the railroad were veterans of the Civil War, from both the North and the South. Some of them shared the Northern values of President Lincoln and other Union leaders, but some just needed a job. Most laborers understood that a transcontinental railroad would reinforce the North's victory over the South by expanding the Union into the West.

## RAILROAD IMAGERY

Railroad imagery was often used in the media as a **metaphor** for President Lincoln's successful attempt to hold the Union together. Lincoln had done a lot of heavy labor in his youth on the American frontier — building fences, clearing the land, and tending crops and livestock. Lincoln became known as "the rail splitter" for splitting logs into rails to build fences. This nickname was used to emphasize his understanding of "the common man."

Lincoln's hard work in his youth prepared him for the even harder work of taking care of his country in dire times.

## GETTING THE JOB DONE

Politics aside, it was time to get the job done. Survey teams were sent out to determine the best routes for the railroads. Careful measurements had to be taken to determine where and how the tracks would be built. Railroad trains travel best on flat surfaces and cannot climb steep hills, which had to be flattened. They needed detailed maps that showed high areas to cut or blast away, and low areas to build up.

## PROPAGANDA

Alongside surveyors and scientists, artists were also important in the creation and selling of the transcontinental railroad. Artists made maps and illustrated advertisements to convince the American public of the railroad's benefits. These advertisements were propaganda, or biased information used to promote a political idea.

**Propaganda similar to this 1942 WWII poster was created to show the benefits of the Union Pacific Railroad.**

## LOST IN TRANSLATION

Coordinators were the middlemen between the engineers and the laborers. They worked with the engineers to make sure the proper construction materials made it to the right place at the right time. They recruited and hired enough men for each of the various jobs and imported Chinese laborers. They sometimes also trained immigrant laborers.

Laborers who worked on the railroad lines had many problems, especially the Chinese immigrants who worked on the Central Pacific line. Most spoke little English and many suffered from "culture shock." They often experienced forms of discrimination, such as low wages. They were initially paid only about $25 to $30 per month for very hard, dangerous labor, and often had trouble collecting their pay.

### FAST FACT

The Chinese language, of which there are many **dialects**, is very different from English. Rather than using an alphabet, written Chinese consists of unique characters for each word. Spoken Chinese depends on pitch (high or low) to distinguish word meaning. These and other differences make it difficult for Chinese speakers to learn English, and for English speakers to learn Chinese.

## DANGER ALL AROUND

The working conditions on the transcontinental railroad were dangerous because the workers had to use nitroglycerin to blast through the mountains to build tunnels. Discovered in the 1840s and developed as a blasting agent in the 1860s, nitroglycerin was very dangerous to handle. The Central Pacific employed chemist James Howden to manufacture nitroglycerin on site, and he was able to make up to 100 pounds (45 kg) of the explosive per day. Using this chemical meant the work was done far faster and more efficiently than cutting through rock with pickaxes. But the efficiency came with a tragic cost.

## DANGEROUS WORKING CONDITIONS

Chinese workers experienced the most extreme form of abuse in the construction of the railroads. Some were lowered in baskets over high cliffs in order to set off explosions. Such working conditions would never be allowed in the United States today.

The train tunnels carved through the Sierra Nevada Mountains were created through the use of explosives such as nitroglycerin.

## LIVING CONDITIONS

Living conditions were dangerous, too, because the workers lived in tents that did not protect them from avalanches and snowslides. Fed up, Chinese workers went on strike on June 25, 1867. Although Charles Crocker raised their pay and cut their hours, they were still not happy. Crocker forced them back to work by cutting off their food supply. It is estimated that between 137 and 1,200 Chinese laborers lost their lives in accidents in the building of the transcontinental railroad. Many more died of diseases such as smallpox.

## CHINESE COMMUNITIES

Many of the Chinese laborers who worked on the transcontinental railroad wanted to earn money and return to China. Others stayed and created vibrant communities in California, most notably in San Francisco.

**San Francisco's Chinatown is the oldest in North America and the largest outside of Asia.**

# THE LAST SPIKE AND LASTING ACHIEVEMENT

For six years, the Central Pacific and the Union Pacific railroads had been charging toward each other from the West and the East to meet their shared destiny. Now, at last, on May 10, 1869, in Promontory Summit in Utah Territory, workers from East and West met. The Last Spike was driven into the rails of America's first transcontinental railroad, joining North America's East and West.

Representatives from the East and West shake hands as the transcontinental railroad is completed.

## AND THE HONOR GOES TO ...

Leland Stanford, one of the "Big Four" who founded the Central Pacific, was given the honor of driving the Last Spike. This was no ordinary spike. David Hewes, a San Francisco businessman, had come up with the idea of using a spike made of gold in order to signify the importance of the event.

## STANFORD UNIVERSITY

Leland Stanford and his wife, Jane, founded Stanford University in 1885. Over the years they donated approximately 40 million dollars to the school, which would be over 1 billion dollars today. Stanford is now considered to be one of the greatest institutes of higher learning in the world.

Stanford University is located 35 miles (56 km) south of San Francisco.

## THE LAST SPIKE

The names of the railroad directors were engraved on the sides of the Last Spike. The date on the golden spike (May 8, 1869) is incorrect because the ceremony had to be put off for two days (to May 10) due to weather problems and labor issues. However, the golden spike was still used. It is now on display at the Cantor Arts Center at Stanford University in California.

### FAST FACT

The Golden Spike National Historic Site offers visitors reenactments of the driving of the Last Spike and allows them to view period-accurate steam locomotives.

The Golden Spike Ceremony was reenacted at the Chicago Railroad Fair in 1949.

## A NEW KIND OF MEDIA EVENT

The people who were actually at the driving of the Last Spike were not the only ones to enjoy the ceremony. Even though radio and television were decades away, this was probably the first "live" media event. The words of the dignitaries at the ceremony were pounded out on telegraph machinery. When the Last Spike was fully driven, the simple message "DONE" flowed through telegraph wires across the nation.

This is a reenactment of the meeting of the engines at the Golden Spike National Historic Site in Utah. This is the location where the Union Pacific and Central Pacific Railroads came together on May 10, 1869.

Morse code used short and long signals—dots and dashes—to represent letters of the alphabet.

## THE TELEGRAPH

The first working telegraph machine was built in 1816 by Francis Ronalds, an English inventor. But it would take decades for others to build on his work and perfect the system. American painter-turned-inventor Samuel Morse was one of the creators of the modern electrical telegraph system and a way to communicate on it: the Morse code.

It is hard for us to imagine how exciting this was to nineteenth-century Americans. Not only did they now have a railroad that could take them from coast to coast, they had the technology that could update them on the latest news in an instant. Though for some the rapid pace of the Industrial Revolution felt overwhelming, most Americans embraced the changes. There was great fanfare across the country at the railroad's completion.

## MANY BENEFITS

The benefits of the first transcontinental railroad were immediately felt by the American public. Travel from coast to coast had previously taken six months or more. Now a person could make the same trip in just one week. The price of traveling across the country was reduced from an average of about $1,000 per person to about $65 (for third class).

## MARKETING

The owners of the railroads knew how to use the most up-to-date marketing strategies to let consumers know how cost-effective and convenient their services were. Along with newspapers, posters were a great way to spread the word.

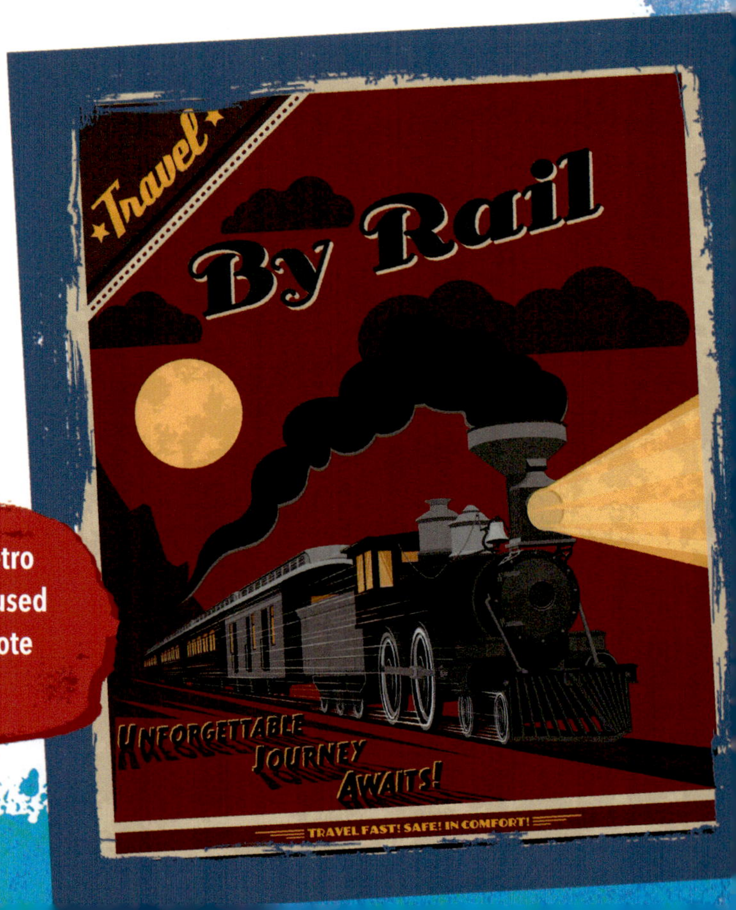


Ads like this retro poster are still used today to promote train travel.

## ECONOMIC BENEFITS

The economic benefits were almost incalculable. From corporate titans to the smallest general store owners, many businessmen were greatly enriched by the transcontinental railroad. Markets for all kinds of businesses grew enormously with expansion into the West. The distribution of products became far cheaper. Production of goods in Eastern factories boomed because of the demand for goods in the West.

The transcontinental railroad delivered many needed supplies to the West.

## THE ONE WHO WASN'T THERE

Having died five years earlier, Theodore Judah couldn't be there on May 10, 1869, to see the realization of his dream — the Last Spike ceremony. But even though the railroad directors tried to minimize his involvement on the day the Last Spike was driven, he is not forgotten today. An 8,245-foot ( 2,513 m) peak in the Sierra Nevada Mountain Range near Donner Pass is named Mount Judah. San Francisco named Judah Street after him, as well as the N-Judah commuter train. An elementary school in Sacramento, California, is also named after Judah.

If only Theodore Judah could have known before he died that his endless efforts to build the first transcontinental railroad were not in vain, and that the memory of "Crazy Judah" would live on.

This monument in Old Sacramento commemorates Theodore Judah for his work on the transcontinental railroad.

# TIMELINE

**1826:** Theodore Judah is born.

**1837–1901:** The Victorian era.

**1846:** The Donner Party becomes trapped in the Sierra Nevada Mountains.

**1848:** The California gold rush begins.

**1854:** William Tecumseh Sherman summons Theodore Judah to New York.

**1856:** Work is completed on the Sacramento Valley railroad line.

**1861:** The American Civil War begins.

**1862:** The Pacific Railroad Act passes the House and Senate, and is signed into law by President Lincoln.

**1863:** Work begins on the transcontinental railroad.

**1863:** Theodore Judah dies in New York City.

**1865:** The American Civil War ends.

**1867:** Chinese workers on the transcontinental railroad go on strike.

**1869:** The transcontinental railroad is completed and the Last Spike is driven.

# GLOSSARY

**boomtown** a town that is experiencing very rapid economic and population growth.

**cannibalism** the eating of human flesh by another human being.

**capitalism** an economic system in which the country's trade and industry are owned by private companies for profit.

**communist** someone who believes in communism, an economic system in which all property is publicly owned and government run.

**dialects** different versions of the same language.

**feudalism** a social system in medieval Europe in which almost all property was owned by the nobility.

**financial sector** the part of the economy that is made up of money markets, banks, and brokers.

**glacial** relating to ice and the changes it can make in Earth's surface.

**ideologies** different thought systems related to economics and politics.

**Industrial Revolution** the rapid development of industry that began in England around 1760 and spread to the rest of the Western world.

**legislators** those who make laws.

**Manifest Destiny** the belief that the expansion of the US throughout the American continent was proper and inevitable.

**metaphor** a thing that is symbolic of something else.

**naïve** showing a lack of maturity and wisdom.

**networking** socializing to further one's business interests.

**resolution** a firm decision to do or not do something.

**Victorian era** the period from 1837 to 1901, when Queen Victoria ruled the British Empire.

# FOR MORE INFORMATION

## Books

Gibson, Karen Bush. *The Oregon Trail: The Journey Across the Country From Lewis and Clark to the Transcontinental Railroad With 25 Projects*. Nomad Press, 2017.

Sandler, Martin. *Iron Rails, Iron Men, and the Race to Link the Nation: The Story of the Transcontinental Railroad*. Candlewick Press, 2015.

Thompson, Linda. *Building the Transcontinental Railroad*. Rourke Educational Media, 2014.

## Websites

Check out the Spike National Historic Site:
**https://www.nps.gov/gosp/index.htm**

Discover more about the history of the transcontinental railroad:
**http://railroad.lindahall.org/essays/black-powder.html**

Learn more about the transcontinental railroad at this interactive site:
**https://www.dkfindout.com/us/history/american-west/transcontinental-railroad/**

# INDEX